Vests, *The long and short*

Whether you want a vest that's elegant or simple, warm and cozy or light and lacy, you are sure to find a great choice in this collection of crochet designs.

LEISURE ARTS, INC. • Maumelle, Arkansas

Fjord Lace

Worked up with a snowflake lace stitch, this piece pays homage to Minnesota's Scandinavian roots. This vest looks stunning whether it is withstanding a breezy fjord or a busy city street. It is finished with a playful fringe.

SHOPPING LIST

EASY

Yarn (Light Weight) 3 LIGHT

[1.75 ounces, 136 yards
(50 grams, 125 meters) per skein]:

- ☐ Main Color (Natural) - 7{8} skeins
- ☐ Color A (Navy) - 1 skein
- ☐ Color B (Pink) - 1 skein

Crochet Hook

- ☐ **Small/Medium:** Size G (4 mm)
- ☐ **Large/Extra Large:** Size 7 (4.5 mm)
  or size needed for gauge

SIZE INFORMATION

Size	Finished Chest Measurement
Small/Medium	34" (86.5 cm)
Large/Extra Large	38" (96.5 cm)

Size Note: We have printed the instructions for the sizes in different colors to make it easier for you to find:

- Size Small/Medium in Blue
- Size Large/Extra Large in Pink

Instructions in Black apply to both sizes.

GAUGE INFORMATION

One Circle Motif thru Rnd 6 = 4{4½}"/10{11.5} cm
One Flower Motif thru Rnd 10 = 4{4½}"/10{11.5} cm

STITCH GUIDE

TREBLE CROCHET ***(abbreviated tr)***

YO twice, insert hook in st indicated, YO and pull up a loop (4 loops on hook), (YO and draw through 2 loops on hook) 3 times.

FIRST CIRCLE MOTIF

Rnd 1 (Right side)**:** With Main Color, ch 5, (dc, ch 1) 7 times in fifth ch from hook **(4 skipped chs count as first dc plus ch 1)**; join with slip st to first dc: 8 dc and 8 ch-1 sps.

Note: Loop a short piece of yarn around any stitch to mark Rnd 1 as **right** side.

Rnd 2: Slip st in first ch-1 sp, ch 3 **(counts as first dc, now and throughout)**, dc in same sp, (ch 2, 2 dc in next ch-1 sp) around, ch 1, sc in first dc to form last ch-2 sp: 16 dc and 8 ch-2 sps.

Rnd 3: Ch 3, dc in last ch-2 sp made, ch 2, (3 dc in next ch-2 sp, ch 2) around, dc in same sp as first dc; join with slip st to first dc: 24 dc and 8 ch-2 sps.

Rnd 4: Ch 1, sc in same st as joining and in next dc, 3 sc in next ch-2 sp, (sc in next 3 dc, 3 sc in next ch-2 sp) around to last dc, sc in last dc; join with slip st to first sc: 48 sc.

Rnd 5: Ch 3, dc in next sc, ch 3, skip next 3 sc, 2 tr in next sc, ch 3, skip next sc, 2 tr in next sc, ch 3, ★ skip next 3 sc, dc in next 3 sc, ch 3, skip next 3 sc, 2 tr in next sc, ch 3, skip next sc, 2 tr in next sc, ch 3; repeat from ★ around to last 4 sc, skip next 3 sc, dc in last sc; join with slip st to first dc: 12 dc, 16 tr, and 12 ch-3 sps.

Rnd 6: Ch 1, sc in same st as joining and in next dc, 5 sc in next ch-3 sp, (sc in next 2 tr, 5 sc in next ch-3 sp) twice, ★ sc in next 3 dc, 5 sc in next ch-3 sp, (sc in next 2 tr, 5 sc in next ch-3 sp) twice; repeat from ★ around to last dc, sc in last dc; join with slip st to first sc: 88 sc.

Rnd 7: Ch 4{6}, slip st in same st as joining and in next 5 sc, ch 4{6}, slip st in next 5 sc, ★ **[**slip st, ch 4{6}, slip st**]** in next sc, slip st in next 5 sc, ch 4{6}, slip st in next 5 sc; repeat from ★ around; join with slip st to joining slip st, finish off: 16 sps.

FLOWER MOTIF

Rnd 1 (Right side)**:** With Main Color, ch 2, 12 sc in second ch from hook; join with slip st to first sc.

Note: Mark Rnd 1 as **right** side.

Rnd 2: Ch 1, 2 sc in Back Loop Only of each sc around ***(Fig. 2, page 30)***; join with slip st to first sc: 24 sc.

Rnd 3: Ch 1, working in Back Loops Only, sc in same st as joining, ch 3, skip next 2 sc, (sc in next sc, ch 3, skip next 2 sc) around; join with slip st to first sc: 8 ch-3 sps.

Rnd 4: Ch 1, (2 sc, 3 dc, 2 sc) in each ch-3 sp around; join with slip st to first sc: 8 petals.

Rnd 5: Working **behind** petals and in Back Loops Only of skipped sc on Rnd 2, sc in first skipped sc below first petal, ch 5, (sc in first skipped sc below next petal, ch 5) around; join with slip st to first sc: 8 ch-5 sps.

Rnd 6: Ch 1, (2 sc, 4 dc, 2 sc) in each ch-5 sp around; join with slip st to first sc: 8 petals.

Rnd 7: (Ch 7, with ch-7 **behind** petal, slip st in first sc on next petal) around, ch 4, dc in first slip st to form last ch-7 sp: 8 ch-7 sps.

Rnd 8: Ch 3, 4 dc in last ch-7 sp made, 9 dc in each ch-7 sp around, 4 dc in same sp as first dc; join with slip st to first dc: 72 dc.

Rnd 9: Ch 1, sc in same st as joining and in next 3 dc, ★ † ch 2, skip next 2 dc, dc in next dc, ch 2, skip next 2 dc, 3 tr in next dc, ch 2, skip next 2 dc, dc in next dc, ch 2, skip next 2 dc †, sc in next 7 dc; repeat from ★ 2 times **more**, then repeat from † to † once, sc in last 3 dc; join with slip st to first sc: 48 sts and 16 ch-2 sps.

Rnd 10: Ch 1, sc in same st as joining and in next 3 sc, ★ † (2 sc in next ch-2 sp, sc in next st) twice, 3 sc in next tr, (sc in next st, 2 sc in next ch-2 sp) twice †, sc in next 7 sc; repeat from ★ 2 times **more**, then repeat from † to † once, sc in last 3 sc; join with slip st to first sc, do **not** finish off: 88 sc.

The method used to connect the Motifs is a no-sew joining also known as "join-as-you-go." After the First Motif is made, each remaining Motif is worked to the last round, then crocheted together as the last round is worked. Holding pieces with **wrong** sides together, slip st in space as indicated ***(Fig. A)***.

Fig. A

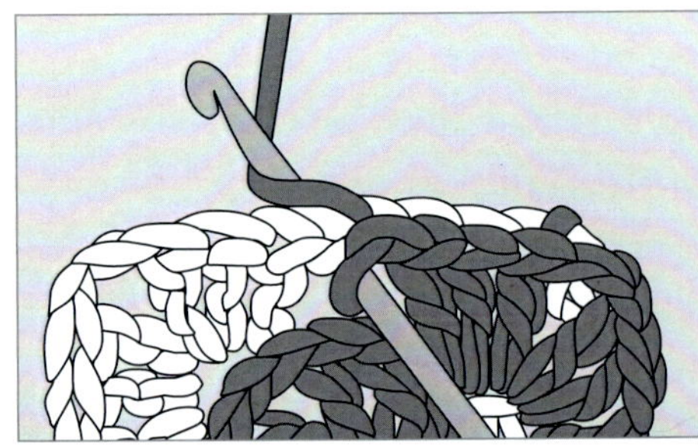

ONE SIDE JOINING

Joining Rnd: Ch 4{6}, slip st in same st as joining and in next 5 sc, ch 4{6}, ★ slip st in next 5 sc, **[**slip st, ch 4{6}, slip st**]** in next sc, slip st in next 5 sc, ch 4{6}; repeat from ★ 3 times **more**, slip st in next 6 sc, ch 2{3}, slip st in corresponding sp on **adjacent Motif**, ch 2{3}, slip st in same sc on **new Motif** and in next 5 sc, † ch 2{3}, slip st in next sp on **adjacent Motif**, ch 2{3}, slip st in next 6 sc on **new Motif**, ch 2{3}, slip st in next sp on **adjacent Motif**, ch 2{3}, slip st in same sc on **new Motif** and in next 5 sc †, repeat from † to † once **more**, ch 4{6}, slip st in last 5 sc; join with slip st to joining slip st, finish off.

REMAINING MOTIFS

Work Circle Motif through Rnd 6, then work One Side Joining to join Circle Motif to Flower Motif.

Using Placement Diagram as a guide, continue to make and join Motifs using One Side or Two Side Joining.

When joining to a previously joined corner, slip st in same space.

TWO SIDE JOINING

Joining Rnd: Ch 4{6}, slip st in same st as joining and in next 5 sc, ch 4{6}, ★ slip st in next 5 sc, [slip st, ch 4{6}, slip st] in next sc, slip st in next 5 sc, ch 4{6}; repeat from ★ once **more**, slip st in next 6 sc, ch 2{3}, slip st in corresponding sp on **adjacent Motif**, ch 2{3}, slip st in same sc on **new Motif** and in next 5 sc, † ch 2{3}, slip st in next sp on **adjacent Motif**, ch 2{3}, slip st in next 6 sc on **new Motif**, ch 2{3}, slip st in next sp on **adjacent Motif**, ch 2{3}, slip st in same sc on **new Motif** and in next 5 sc †, repeat from † to † 3 times **more**, ch 4{6}, slip st in last 5 sc; join with slip st to joining slip st, finish off.

TWO OPPOSITE SIDES JOINING

Joining Rnd: Ch 4{6}, slip st in same st as joining and in next 5 sc, † ch 4{6}, slip st in next 6 sc, ch 2{3}, slip st in corresponding sp on **adjacent Motif**, ch 2{3}, slip st in same sc on **new Motif** and in next 5 sc, ★ ch 2{3}, slip st in next sp on **adjacent Motif**, ch 2{3}, slip st in next 6 sc on **new Motif**, ch 2{3}, slip st in next sp on **adjacent Motif**, ch 2{3}, slip st in same sc on **new Motif** and in next 5 sc; repeat from ★ once **more**, ch 4{6}, slip st in next 5 sc †, [slip st, ch 4{6}, slip st] in next sc, slip st in next 5 sc, repeat from † to † once; join with slip st to joining slip st, finish off.

FINISHING

Block vest to finished measurement *(see Blocking, page 31)*.

ARMHOLE EDGING

Rnd 1: With **right** side facing, join Color A with sc in center ch-4{6} sp at bottom of armhole edge ***(see Joining With Sc, page 30)***; ch 5, [sc in next ch-4{6} sp, ch 5] around; join with slip st to first sc, finish off.

Rnd 2: With **right** side facing, join Color B with sc in same sc as joining; ch 5, (sc in next sc, ch 5) around; join with slip st to first sc, finish off.

Rnd 3: With Main Color, repeat Rnd 2.

Rnd 4: Repeat Rnd 2.

Rnd 5: With Color A, repeat Rnd 2.

Repeat for second Armhole.

BODY EDGING

Joining Color A with sc in center ch-4{6} sp at bottom edge of back, work same as Armhole Edging around outer edge of vest.

FRINGE

Holding three, 14" (35.5 cm) strands of each color together, add fringe in each ch-5 sp across bottom edge ***(Figs. 7a & b, page 31)***.

PLACEMENT DIAGRAM

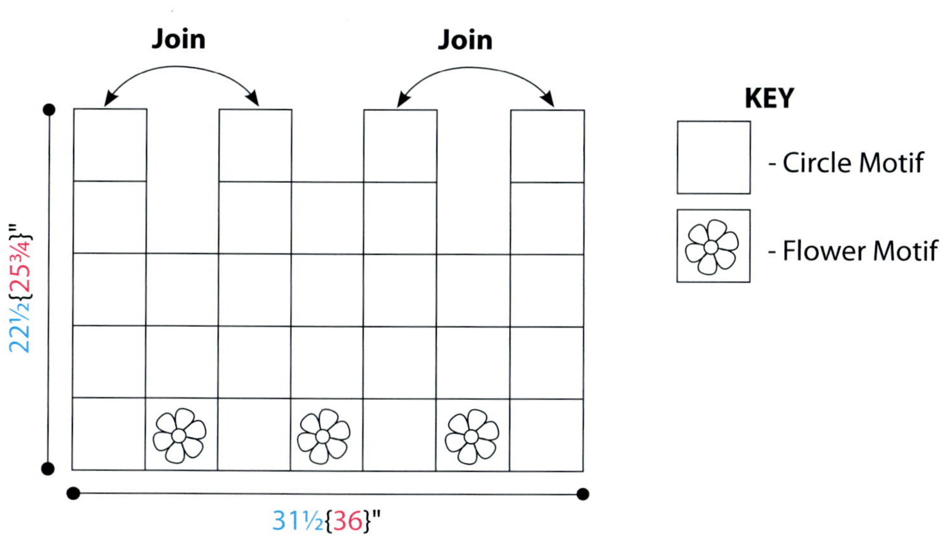

Cherry Schwinn

This wrapped vest is worked up in the Catherine Wheels pattern, a stitch reminiscent of bicycle wheels. The three asymmetrical panels hug the body just right making this a flattering style on any type.

SHOPPING LIST EASY

Yarn (Light Weight) LIGHT 3

[1.75 ounces, 161 yards (50 grams, 147 meters) per skein]:

☐ 8{9-10-11} skeins

Crochet Hook

☐ Size I (5.5 mm) **or** size needed for gauge

Additional Supplies

☐ Tapestry needle

SIZE INFORMATION

Size	Finished Chest Measurement	
Small	32"	(81.5 cm)
Medium	36"	(91.5 cm)
Large	41"	(104 cm)
Extra Large	45"	(114.5 cm)

Size Note: We have printed the instructions for the sizes in different colors to make it easier for you to find:

- Size Small in Blue
- Size Medium in Pink
- Size Large in Green
- Size Extra Large in Brown

Instructions in Black apply to all sizes.

GAUGE INFORMATION

9 hdc = 2½" (6.25 cm)
In pattern,
2 repeats (20 sts) = 4½" (11.5 cm),
8 rows = 4" (10 cm)
Gauge Swatch: 6" wide x 4" high
(15.25 cm x 10 cm)
Ch 27.
Work same as Back through Row 8: 8 sc and 3 dc groups.
Finish off.

STITCH GUIDE

3-DC CLUSTER (uses next 3 sts)
★ YO, insert hook in **next** st, YO and pull up a loop, YO and draw through 2 loops on hook; repeat from ★ 2 times **more**, YO and draw through all 4 loops on hook.
4-DC CLUSTER (uses next 4 sts)
★ YO, insert hook in **next** st, YO and pull up a loop, YO and draw through 2 loops on hook; repeat from ★ 3 times **more**, YO and draw through all 5 loops on hook.
7-DC CLUSTER (uses next 7 sts)
★ YO, insert hook in **next** st, YO and pull up a loop, YO and draw through 2 loops on hook; repeat from ★ 6 times **more**, YO and draw through all 8 loops on hook.

BACK

Ch 67{77-87-97}.

Row 1 (Right side)**:** Sc in second ch from hook and in each ch across: 66{76-86-96} sc.

Note: Loop a short piece of yarn around any stitch to mark Row 1 as **right** side **and** top edge.

Row 2: Ch 1, turn; sc in first 2 sc, ★ skip next 3 sc, 7 dc in next sc, skip next 3 sc, sc in next 3 sc; repeat from ★ across to last 4 sc, skip next 3 sc, 4 dc in last sc: 20{23-26-29} sc and 7{8-9-10} dc groups.

Row 3: Ch 1, turn; sc in first 2 dc, ch 3, ★ work 7-dc Cluster, ch 3, sc in next 3 dc, ch 3; repeat from ★ across to last 4 sts, work 4-dc Cluster: 20{23-26-29} sc and 7{8-9-10} Clusters.

Row 4: Ch 3 **(counts as first dc, now and throughout)**, turn; 3 dc in first st, skip next sp, ★ sc in next 3 sc, skip next sp, 7 dc in next Cluster, skip next sp; repeat from ★ across to last 2 sc, sc in last 2 sc: 20{23-26-29} sc and 7{8-9-10} dc groups.

Row 5: Ch 3, turn; work 3-dc Cluster, ch 3, ★ sc in next 3 dc, ch 3, work 7-dc Cluster, ch 3; repeat from ★ across to last 2 dc, sc in last 2 dc: 20{23-26-29} sc and 7{8-9-10} Clusters.

Row 6: Ch 1, turn; sc in first 2 sc, skip next sp, ★ 7 dc in next Cluster, skip next sp, sc in next 3 sc, skip next sp; repeat from ★ across to last Cluster, 4 dc in last Cluster: 20{23-26-29} sc and 7{8-9-10} dc groups.

Repeat Rows 3-6 for pattern until Back measures approximately 18{18-20-20}"/45.5{45.5-51-51} cm from beginning ch, ending by working a **wrong** side row; do **not** finish off.

EDGING

Row 1: Do **not** turn; sc evenly across end of rows; working in free loops of beginning ch *(Fig. 3, page 30)*, 3 sc in ch at base of first sc, sc in each ch across to last ch, 3 sc in last ch; sc evenly across end of rows, leave bottom edge unworked.

Row 2: Ch 1, turn; sc in each sc around working 3 sc in center sc of each corner 3-sc group; finish off.

RIGHT FRONT

Ch 57{67-77-87}.

Work same as Back until Right Front measures approximately 20{20-22-22}"/51{51-56-56} cm from beginning ch, ending by working a **wrong** side row; do **not** finish off: 17{20-23-26} sc and 6{7-8-9} dc groups.

Work Edging same as Back.

LEFT FRONT

Ch 57{67-77-87}.

Work same as Back until Left Front measures approximately 22{22-24-24}"/56{56-61-61} cm from beginning ch, ending by working a **wrong** side row; do **not** finish off: 17{20-23-26} sc and 6{7-8-9} dc groups.

Work Edging same as Back.

FINISHING

Block Back and Fronts *(**see Blocking, page 31**)*.

SHOULDER SEAMS

With **right** sides of Left Front and Back together, matching top edges (beginning ch), and working through both pieces, join yarn with slip st in first st at side edge, slip st in next 9 sts; finish off.

Join Right Front to Back in same manner.

SIDE SEAMS

With **right** sides of Right Front and Back together, leaving first 7{7½-8-8½}"/18{19-20.5-21.5} cm from shoulder seam unworked for armhole and working through inside loops of sc on Edging on both pieces, join yarn with slip st in next sc; slip st in each sc across side edge to join pieces, leaving the extra 2" (5 cm) length on the Front unworked.

Join Left Front to Back in same manner, leaving the extra 4" (10 cm) length on the Front unworked.

ARMHOLE EDGING

With **right** side facing, join yarn with slip st at side seam; slip st in each sc around; join with slip st to first slip st, finish off.

Repeat for second Armhole.

COLLAR

Row 1: With **right** side facing, join yarn with slip st in first st on top edge of Right Front; ch 2 **(counts as first hdc, now and throughout)**, hdc in each st across Right Front, Back, and Left Front.

Rows 2-14: Ch 2, turn; hdc in each hdc across.

Finish off.

Placing Right Front over Left Front, sew corner of each Front to shoulder of opposite Front.

Irish Mist

Using a bulky weight yarn, you can whip this baby up over the weekend. This vest is fitted through the waistline making it a flattering addition to your wardrobe. Wearing this vest will be like wrapping yourself in a comforting embrace on a cool misty morning.

SHOPPING LIST

EASY

Yarn (Bulky Weight) BULKY 5

[3.5 ounces, 90 yards (100 grams, 82.3 meters) per skein]:

☐ 6{7-7-8} skeins

Crochet Hook

☐ Size L (8 mm) **or** size needed for gauge

Additional Supplies

☐ Yarn needle

SIZE INFORMATION

Size	Finished Chest Measurement
Small	34" (86.5 cm)
Medium	36" (91.5 cm)
Large	38" (96.5 cm)
Extra Large	40" (101.5 cm)

Size Note: We have printed the instructions for the sizes in different colors to make it easier for you to find:

- Size Small in Blue
- Size Medium in Pink
- Size Large in Green
- Size Extra Large in Brown

Instructions in Black apply to all sizes.

GAUGE INFORMATION

In pattern,
7 sts = 3¼" (8.25 cm),
8 rows = 3½" (9 cm)

Gauge Swatch: 3¼" wide x 3½" high (8.25 cm x 9 cm)

Ch 8.

Row 1: Sc in second ch from hook and in each ch across: 7 sc.

Row 2: Ch 1, turn; working in both loops, sc in first sc, (dc in next sc, sc in next sc) across.

Row 3: Ch 1, turn; sc in Front Loop Only of each st across ***(Fig. 2, page 30)***.

Rows 4-8: Repeat Rows 2 and 3 twice, then repeat Row 2 once **more**. Finish off.

STITCH GUIDE

TREBLE CROCHET *(abbreviated tr)*
YO twice, insert hook in st indicated, YO and pull up a loop (4 loops on hook), (YO and draw through 2 loops on hook) 3 times.

SINGLE CROCHET 2 TOGETHER *(abbreviated sc2tog)*
Pull up a loop in each of next 2 sts, YO and draw through all 3 loops on hook (**counts as one sc**).

BODY (Make 2)

Ch 38{40-42-44}.

Row 1 (Right side)**:** Sc in back ridge of second ch from hook and in each ch across ***(Fig. 1, page 30)***: 37{39-41-43} sc.

Note: Loop a short piece of yarn around any stitch to mark Row 1 as **right** side.

Row 2: Ch 1, turn; sc in Front Loop Only of each sc across ***(Fig. 2, page 30)***.

Row 3: Ch 1, turn; working in both loops, sc in first sc, (dc in next sc, sc in next sc) across.

Row 4: Ch 1, turn; sc in Front Loop Only of each st across.

Row 5: Ch 1, turn; working in both loops, sc in first sc, (dc in next sc, sc in next sc) across.

Row 6 (Decrease row)**:** Ch 1, turn; working in Front Loops Only and beginning in first sc, sc2tog, sc in each st across to last 2 sts, sc2tog: 35{37-39-41} sc.

Rows 7-13: Repeat Rows 3-6 once, then repeat Rows 3-5 once **more**: 33{35-37-39} sc.

Row 14 (Increase row)**:** Ch 1, turn; working in Front Loops Only, 2 sc in first sc, sc in each st across to last st, 2 sc in last sc: 35{37-39-41} sc.

Rows 15-17: Repeat Rows 3-5.

Row 18: Repeat Row 14: 37{39-41-43} sc.

Rows 19 thru 27{29-31-33}: Repeat Row 3, then repeat Rows 4 and 5, 4{5-6-7} times.

Place a marker around first and last sc on last row to mark beginning of armhole.

ARMHOLE SHAPING

Row 1 (Decrease row)**:** Ch 1, turn; working in Front Loops Only and beginning in first sc, sc2tog, sc in each st across to last 2 sts, sc2tog: 35{37-39-41} sc.

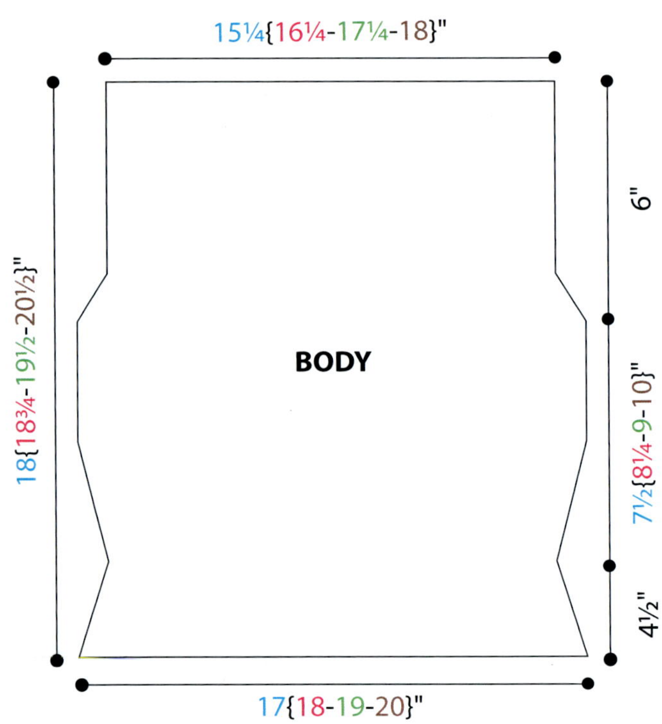

Row 2: Ch 1, turn; working in both loops, sc in first sc, (dc in next sc, sc in next sc) across.

Row 3: Repeat Row 1: 33{35-37-39} sc.

Rows 4-14: Work across in established pattern.

Finish off.

FINISHING

SHOULDER SEAMS

With **wrong** sides of each Body together, sew shoulder seams across 4 sts on each side using mattress stitch and working under top 2 loops to form 2 lines of sts *(Figs. 6a & b, page 31)*.

SIDE EDGING

With **right** sides facing and beginning at bottom edge, join yarn with slip st in first row; slip st in end of each row across; finish off.

Repeat for second side.

SIDE SEAMS

With **wrong** sides of each Body together and beginning at bottom edge, sew seam to markers using mattress stitch and working under top 2 loops of sts to form 2 lines of sts.

Repeat for second side.

COWL NECK

Rnd 1: With **right** side facing, join yarn with slip st in first st on neck edge; ch 4 **(counts as first tr, now and throughout)**, tr in next st and in each st around; join with slip st to first tr: 50{54-58-62} tr.

Rnds 2-6: Ch 4, tr in next tr and in each tr around; join with slip st to first tr.

Rnds 7-10: Ch 1, sc in Back Loop Only of each st around; join with slip st to first sc.

Rnd 11: Slip st in Back Loop Only of each sc around; join with slip st to first slip st, finish off.

Café Au Lait
Cable Wrap

The color of this wrap reminds me of a perfectly steaming cup of cafe au lait, and it plays well with coffee dates of all varieties. Try it with an old friend, a new acquaintance, a romance, or even the pages of a good book. You can wear this easy textured wrap vest alone or layered with longer sleeves for a cozy and chic pullover.

SHOPPING LIST

EASY

Yarn (Bulky Weight) BULKY 5

[3.5 ounces, 120 yards (100 grams, 109 meters) per skein**]**:

- ☐ 7{8-8-9} skeins

Crochet Hook

- ☐ Size M/N (9 mm) **or** size needed for gauge

Additional Supplies

- ☐ Sewing needle and thread
- ☐ 1¼" (32 mm) Buttons - 2

SIZE INFORMATION

Size	Finished Chest Measurement	
Small	32"	(81.5 cm)
Medium	36"	(91.5 cm)
Large	40"	(101.5 cm)
Extra Large	44"	(112 cm)

Size Note: We have printed the instructions for the sizes in different colors to make it easier for you to find:

- Size Small in Blue
- Size Medium in Pink
- Size Large in Green
- Size Extra Large in Brown

Instructions in Black apply to all sizes.

GAUGE INFORMATION

In pattern, 8 sts and 6 rows = 4" (10 cm)

Gauge Swatch: 4" (10 cm) square

Ch 9.

Row 1: Sc in second ch from hook and in each ch across: 8 sc.

Row 2: Ch 3, turn; work beginning Linked dc ***(Fig. A)***, dc in next sc and in each sc across.

Row 3: Ch 1, turn; sc in each st across.

Rows 4-6: Repeat Rows 2 and 3 once, then repeat Row 2 once **more**.

Finish off.

STITCH GUIDE

BEGINNING LINKED DOUBLE CROCHET

(abbreviated beginning Linked dc)

Pull up a loop in second ch from hook and in next sc ***(Fig. A)***, (YO and draw through 2 loops on hook) twice.

Fig. A

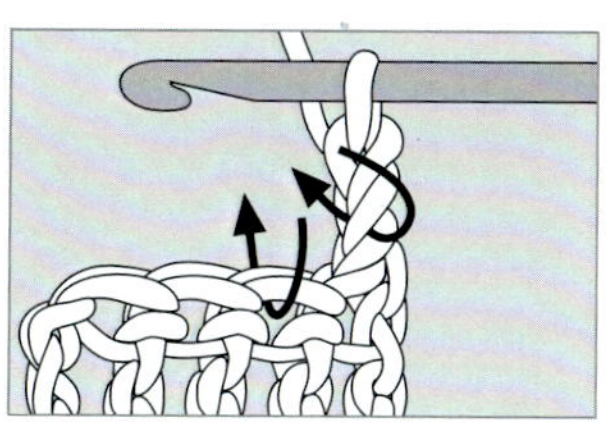

FRONT POST TREBLE CROCHET

(abbreviated FPtr)

YO twice, insert hook from **front** to **back** around post of st indicated ***(Fig. 4, page 30)***, YO and pull up a loop (4 loops on hook), (YO and draw through 2 loops on hook) 3 times.

DOUBLE CROCHET 2 TOGETHER

(abbreviated dc2tog) (uses 2 chs)

★ YO, insert hook in ch indicated, YO and pull up a loop, YO and draw through 2 loops on hook; repeat from ★ once **more**, YO and draw through all 3 loops on hook **(counts as one dc)**.

BACK

Ch 31{33-35-37}.

Row 1 (Right side)**:** Sc in second ch from hook and in each ch across: 30{32-34-36} sc.

Note: Loop a short piece of yarn around any stitch to mark Row 1 **right** side **and** top edge.

Row 2: Ch 3 **(counts as first dc, now and throughout)**, turn; work beginning Linked dc, dc in next 10{11-12-13} sc, place marker around last dc made, dc in next sc and in each sc across.

Row 3: Ch 1, turn; sc in each st across.

Row 4: Ch 3, turn; work beginning Linked dc, dc in next 7{8-9-10} sc, beginning with marked dc in row **below** sc row, work FPtr around each of next 4 dc, skip 4 sc **behind** FPtr just made, dc in next 4 sc, work FPtr around each of next 4 dc in row **below** sc row, skip 4 sc **behind** FPtr just made, dc in last 9{10-11-12} sc.

Row 5: Ch 1, turn; sc in each st across.

Row 6: Ch 3, turn; work beginning Linked dc, dc in next 7{8-9-10} sc, work FPtr around each of next 4 FPtr in row **below** sc row, skip 4 sc **behind** FPtr just made, dc in next 4 sc, work FPtr around each of next 4 FPtr in row **below** sc row, skip 4 sc **behind** FPtr just made, dc in last 9{10-11-12} sc.

Row 7: Ch 1, turn; sc in each st across.

Row 8: Ch 3, turn; work beginning Linked dc, dc in next 9{10-11-12} sc, work FPtr around each of next 8 FPtr in row **below** sc row, skip 8 sc **behind** FPtr, dc in last 11{12-13-14} sc.

Row 9: Ch 1, turn; sc in each st across.

Rows 10 and 11: Repeat Rows 8 and 9.

Row 12: Ch 3, turn; work beginning Linked dc, dc in next 7{8-9-10} sc, work FPtr around each of next 4 FPtr in row **below** sc row, skip 4 sc **behind** FPtr just made, dc in next 4 sc, work FPtr around each of next 4 FPtr in row **below** sc row, skip 4 sc **behind** FPtr just made, dc in last 9{10-11-12} sc.

Rows 13-35: Repeat Rows 5-12 twice, then repeat Rows 5-11 once **more**.

Finish off.

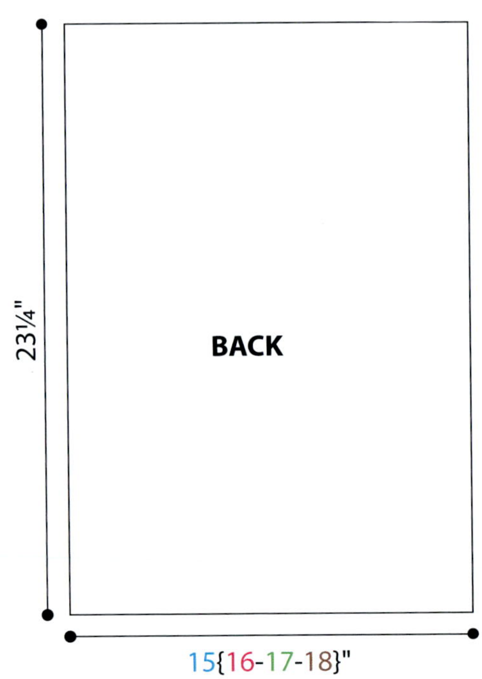

RIGHT FRONT

Ch 31{35-39-43}.

Row 1 (Wrong side)**:** Sc in second ch from hook and in each ch across: 30{34-38-42} sc.

Note: Loop a short piece of yarn around the **back** of any stitch on Row 1 to mark **right** side **and** top edge.

Row 2: Ch 3, turn; work beginning Linked dc, dc in next sc and in each sc across.

Row 3: Ch 1, turn; sc in each st across.

Rows 4-35: Repeat Rows 2 and 3, 16 times.

Finish off.

LEFT FRONT

Ch 31{35-39-43}.

Row 1: Sc in second ch from hook and in each ch across: 30{34-38-42} sc.

Row 2 (Right side)**:** Ch 3, turn; work beginning Linked dc, dc in next sc and in each sc across.

Note: Mark Row 2 as **right** side **and** top edge.

Row 3: Ch 1, turn; sc in each st across.

Row 4: Ch 3, turn; work beginning Linked dc, dc in next 3 dc, work FPtr around each of next 2 dc in row **below** sc row, skip 2 sc **behind** FPtr, dc in next 4 sc, skip next 4 dc from last FPtr made in row **below** sc row and work FPtr around each of next 2 dc, skip 2 sc **behind** FPtr, dc in next sc and in each sc across.

Row 5: Ch 1, turn; sc in each st across.

Row 6: Ch 3, turn; work beginning Linked dc, dc in next 3 dc, work FPtr around each of next 2 FPtr in row **below** sc row, skip 2 sc **behind** FPtr, dc in next 4 sc, work FPtr around each of next 2 FPtr in row **below** sc row, skip 2 sc **behind** FPtr, dc in next sc and in each sc across.

Row 7: Ch 1, turn; sc in each st across.

Rows 8-35: Repeat Rows 6 and 7, 14 times.

Finish off.

FINISHING

SIDE SEAMS

With **right** sides of Left Front and Back together and matching bottom edges (last row made), join yarn with slip st in bottom corner; slip st evenly across end of rows to join pieces, leaving last 7{7½-8-8½}"/18{19-20.5-21.5} cm unworked for armhole.

Join Right Front to Back in same manner.

COLLAR

Row 1: With **right** side facing and working in free loops of beginning ch ***(Fig. 3, page 30)***, join yarn with slip st in ch at base of first sc on Right Front; ch 3, work beginning Linked dc, dc in next ch and in each ch across to last ch, working in last ch on Right Front **and** in ch at base of first sc on Back, dc2tog, dc in next ch and in each ch across Back to last ch, working in last ch on Back **and** in ch at base of first sc on Left Front, dc2tog, dc in next ch and in each ch across:
88{98-108-118} sts.

Row 2: Ch 1, turn; sc in each st across.

Row 3: Ch 3, turn; work beginning Linked dc, dc in next sc and in each sc across.

Rows 4-10: Repeat Rows 2 and 3, 3 times; then repeat Row 2 once **more**.

Finish off.

Sew buttons to Row 2 of Right Front, 2 sts from each edge. Use spaces on edge of Left Front for buttonholes.

Starburst Duster

This long, fitted vest can be worked up in yummy silk yarn, resulting in an exotic duster with a flattering drape. The back shows off a starburst pattern.

SHOPPING LIST

EASY +

Yarn (Light Weight) LIGHT 3

[2.2 ounces, 102 yards (65 grams, 93 meters) per ball]:

☐ 6{8} balls

Crochet Hook

☐ Size G (4 mm) **or** size needed for gauge

Additional Supplies

☐ Tapestry needle

SIZE INFORMATION

Size	Finished Chest Measurement
Small/Medium	34" (86.5 cm)
Large/Extra Large	38" (96.5 cm)

Size Note: We have printed the instructions for the sizes in different colors to make it easier for you to find:

- Size Small/Medium in Blue
- Size Large/Extra Large in Pink

Instructions in Black apply to both sizes.

GAUGE INFORMATION

16 dc and 8 rows = 4" (10 cm)

Gauge Swatch: 4" (10 cm) square

Ch 18.

Row 1: Dc in fourth ch from hook **(3 skipped chs count as first dc)** and in each ch across: 16 dc.

Rows 2-8: Ch 3 **(counts as first dc)**, turn; dc in next dc and in each dc across.

Finish off.

STITCH GUIDE

DOUBLE CROCHET 2 TOGETHER

(abbreviated dc2tog) (uses next 2 sts)

★ YO, insert hook in **next** st, YO and pull up a loop, YO and draw through 2 loops on hook; repeat from ★ once **more**, YO and draw through all 3 loops on hook **(counts as one dc)**.

The Body is worked in one piece, with an opening for the Motif to be sewn to the back. The last row on each Front is sewn to the top edge of the Motif to form the armholes.

MOTIF

Ch 4; join with slip st to form a ring.

Rnd 1 (Right side)**:** Ch 5 **(counts as first dc plus ch 2)**, (3 dc in ring, ch 2) 3 times, 2 dc in ring; join with slip st to first dc: 12 dc and 4 ch-2 sps.

Note: Loop a short piece of yarn around any stitch to mark Rnd 1 as **right** side.

Rnd 2: Slip st in first ch-2 sp, ch 7 **(counts as first dc plus ch 4)**, 2 dc in same sp, dc in next dc, ch 1, skip next dc, dc in next dc, ★ (2 dc, ch 4, 2 dc) in next ch-2 sp, dc in next dc, ch 1, skip next dc, dc in next dc; repeat from ★ 2 times **more**, dc in same sp as first dc; join with slip st to first dc: 24 dc and 8 sps.

Rnds 3-11: Slip st in first ch-4 sp, ch 7, 2 dc in same sp, dc in each dc across to next ch-1 sp, ch 1, skip next ch-1 sp, dc in each dc across to next corner ch-4 sp, ★ (2 dc, ch 4, 2 dc) in corner ch-4 sp, dc in each dc across to next ch-1 sp, ch 1, skip next ch-1 sp, dc in each dc across to next corner ch-4 sp; repeat from ★ 2 times **more**, dc in same sp as first dc; join with slip st to first dc: 168 dc and 8 sps.

Rnd 12: Slip st in first ch-4 sp, ch 1, 6 sc in same sp, sc in each dc and in each ch-1 sp around working 6 sc in each corner ch-4 sp; join with slip st to first sc: 196 sc.

Rnd 13: Slip st in each st around; finish off.

BODY

Ch 131{151}.

Row 1 (Right side)**:** Sc in second ch from hook and in each ch across: 130{150} sc.

Note: Mark Row 1 as **right** side.

Row 2: Ch 3 **(counts as first dc, now and throughout)**, turn; dc in next 9 sc, ★ ch 1, (skip next sc, dc in next sc, ch 1) 4 times, skip next sc, dc in next 11 sc; repeat from ★ across: 7{8} solid blocks and 6{7} mesh blocks.

Rows 3-5: Ch 3, turn; dc in next 9 dc, ★ (ch 1, skip next dc, dc in next ch) 5 times, dc in next 10 dc; repeat from ★ across.

Row 6: Ch 4 **(counts as first dc plus ch 1, now and throughout)**, turn; (skip next dc, dc in next dc, ch 1) 4 times, skip next dc, (dc in next dc, dc in next ch) 5 times, ★ † ch 1, (skip next dc, dc in next dc, ch 1) 4 times, skip next dc †, dc in next 2 dc, dc in next ch, (dc in next dc, dc in next ch) 4 times; repeat from ★ across to last 10 dc, then repeat from † to † once, dc in last dc: 6{7} solid blocks and 7{8} mesh blocks.

Rows 7-9: Ch 4, turn; (skip next ch, dc in next dc, ch 1) 4 times, skip next ch, dc in next 10 dc, ★ (ch 1, skip next dc, dc in next ch) 5 times, dc in next 10 dc; repeat from ★ across to last 5 ch-1 sps, (ch 1, skip next ch, dc in next dc) 5 times.

Row 10: Ch 3, turn; dc in next ch, (dc in next dc, dc in next ch) 4 times, ★ † ch 1, (skip next dc, dc in next dc, ch 1) 4 times, skip next dc †, dc in next 2 dc, dc in next ch, (dc in next dc, dc in next ch) 4 times; repeat from ★ across to last 2 blocks, then repeat from † to † once, dc in next dc, (dc in next ch, dc in next dc) 5 times: 7{8} solid blocks and 6{7} mesh blocks.

Rows 11-33: Repeat Rows 3-10 twice, then repeat Rows 3-9 once **more**.

LEFT FRONT

SIZE SMALL/MEDIUM ONLY

Row 1: Ch 3, turn; dc in next ch, (dc in next dc, dc in next ch) 4 times, ch 1, (skip next dc, dc in next dc, ch 1) 4 times, skip next dc, dc in next 2 dc, dc in next ch, (dc in next dc, dc in next ch) 4 times, (ch 1, skip next dc, dc in next dc) 5 times, leave remaining sts unworked: 2 solid blocks and 2 mesh blocks.

SIZE LARGE/EXTRA LARGE ONLY

Row 1: Ch 3, turn; dc in next ch, (dc in next dc, dc in next ch) 4 times, ★ ch 1, (skip next dc, dc in next dc, ch 1) 4 times, skip next dc, dc in next 2 dc, dc in next ch, (dc in next dc, dc in next ch) 4 times; repeat from ★ once **more**, leave remaining sts unworked: 3 solid blocks and 2 mesh blocks.

BOTH SIZES

Maintain established pattern throughout.

Next 7 Rows: Work even.

Next 5 Rows: Work dc2tog twice at **each** edge: 20{30} sts.

Next 4{9} Rows: Work dc2tog twice at neck edge only: 12 sts.

Next Row: Work dc2tog once at neck edge only: 11 sts.

Next 18{17} Rows: Work even.

Finish off.

RIGHT FRONT

SIZE SMALL/MEDIUM ONLY

Row 1: With **wrong** side facing, skip 50 sts from Left Front and join yarn with dc in next dc ***(see Joining With Dc, page 30)***; ★ ch 1, (skip next dc, dc in next dc, ch 1) 4 times, skip next dc, (dc in next dc, dc in next ch) 5 times; repeat from ★ once **more**, dc in last dc: 2 solid blocks and 2 mesh blocks.

SIZE LARGE/EXTRA LARGE ONLY

Row 1: With **wrong** side facing, skip 50 sts from Left Front and join yarn with dc in next dc ***(see Joining With Dc, page 30)***; † dc in next ch, (dc in next dc, dc in next ch) 4 times, ch 1, (skip next dc, dc in next dc, ch 1) 4 times, skip next dc †, dc in next 2 dc, repeat from † to † once, dc in next dc, (dc in next ch, dc in next dc) 5 times: 3 solid blocks and 2 mesh blocks.

BOTH SIZES

Complete same as Left Front.

FINISHING

Using photo as a guide for placement, with **wrong** sides together, whipstitch Motif to Body ***(Figs. 5a & b, page 30)***.

Whipstitch top edges of Fronts to top edge of Motif.

ARMHOLE EDGINGS

With **right** side facing and working across end of rows on Front Armhole, join yarn with slip st in first row; ch 2, (sc, ch 2) evenly across to last row, slip st in last row; finish off.

Repeat for second Armhole.

BODY EDGING

With **right** side facing and working across end of rows on Right Front, join yarn with slip st in bottom corner; ch 2, (sc, ch 2) evenly across end of rows to beginning of neck shaping; ch 71 (for tie), slip st in second ch from hook and in each ch across; ch 2, (sc, ch 2) evenly across to last row, slip st in last row; finish off.

With **right** side facing and working across end of rows on Left Front, join yarn with slip st in first row; ch 2, (sc, ch 2) evenly across to end of neck shaping; ch 71 (for tie), slip st in second ch from hook and in each ch across; ch 2, (sc, ch 2) evenly across to bottom corner, slip st in corner; finish off.

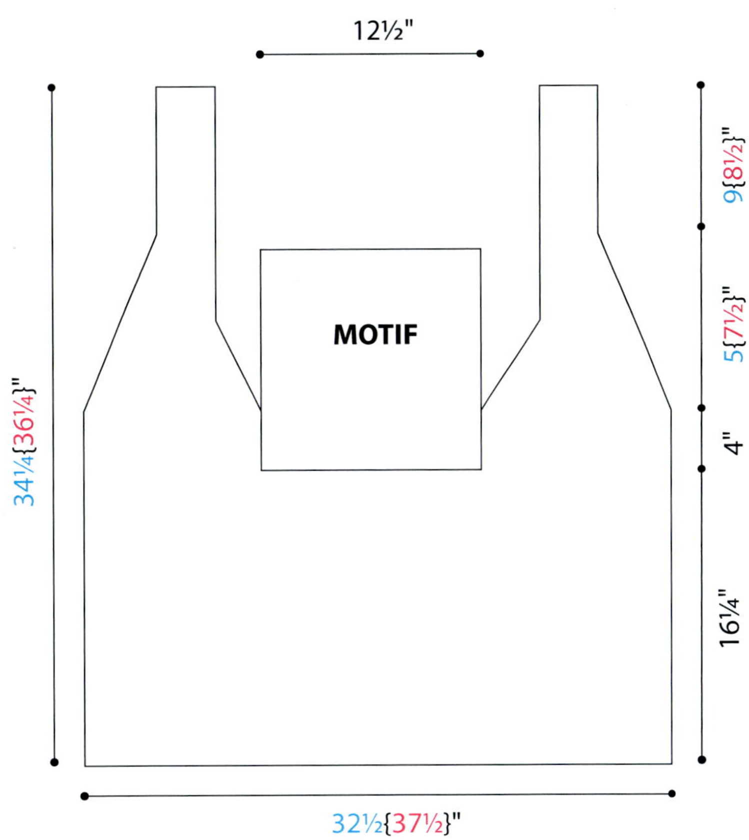

Tidal Wave

This vest is perfect for a night on the town. Worked up in subtle lace and post stitches with a variegated yarn and finished with a lacy edging, this lovely A-line vest will make a splash on any occasion.

SHOPPING LIST

EASY

Yarn (Light Weight) LIGHT 3

[3.5 ounces, 290 yards (100 grams, 265.2 meters) per skein]:

☐ 3{3-4-4} skeins

Crochet Hook

☐ Size G (4 mm) **or** size needed for gauge

SIZE INFORMATION

Sizes	Top Width	Bottom Width
Small	13" (33 cm)	16½" (42 cm)
Medium	14½" (37 cm)	18" (45.5 cm)
Large	16" (40.5 cm)	19½" (49.5 cm)
Extra Large	17½" (44.5 cm)	21" (53.5 cm)

Size Note: We have printed the instructions for the sizes in different colors to make it easier for you to find:

- Size Small in Blue
- Size Medium in Pink
- Size Large in Green
- Size Extra Large in Brown

Instructions in Black apply to all sizes.

GAUGE INFORMATION

In pattern,
19 hdc = 4" (10 cm),
2 repeats (12 rows) = 4¼" (10.75 cm)

Gauge Swatch: 4" (10 cm) wide

Ch 20.

Row 1: Hdc in third ch from hook **(2 skipped chs count as first hdc)** and in each ch across: 19 hdc.

Rows 2-6: Ch 2 **(does not count as a st)**, turn; hdc in each hdc across.

Finish off.

STITCH GUIDE

TREBLE CROCHET *(abbreviated tr)*

YO twice, insert hook in st indicated, YO and pull up a loop (4 loops on hook), (YO and draw through 2 loops on hook) 3 times.

FRONT POST TREBLE CROCHET *(abbreviated FPtr)*

YO twice, insert hook from **front** to **back** around post of st indicated ***(Fig. 4, page 30)***, YO and pull up a loop (4 loops on hook), (YO and draw through 2 loops on hook) 3 times.

HALF DOUBLE CROCHET 2 TOGETHER *(abbreviated hdc2tog)* (uses first 2 sts)

YO, insert hook in first st, YO and pull up a loop, YO, insert hook in next st, YO and pull up a loop, YO and draw through all 5 loops on hook **(counts as one hdc)**.

BODY (Make 2)

Ch 71{79-87-95}.

Row 1: Sc in second ch from hook and in each ch across: 70{78-86-94} sc.

Row 2 (Right side)**:** Ch 2 **(does not count as a st)**, turn; hdc2tog, (ch 2, skip next 2 sc, hdc in next 2 sc) 8{9-10-11} times, 2 hdc in next sc, hdc in next 2 sc, place marker in last hdc made, hdc in next sc, (ch 2, skip next 2 sc, hdc in next 2 sc) across: 38{42-46-50} hdc and 16{18-20-22} ch-2 sps.

Note: Loop a short piece of yarn around any stitch to mark Row 2 as **right** side **and** top edge.

Row 3: Ch 2, turn; hdc2tog, hdc in each ch and in each hdc across to marked st, remove marker, ch 2, skip next 2 hdc, 2 hdc in next hdc, ch 2, skip next 2 hdc, hdc in each hdc and in each ch across: 66{74-82-90} hdc and 2 ch-2 sps.

Row 4: Ch 2, turn; hdc2tog, hdc in each hdc and in each ch across to center 2-hdc group, ch 3, skip center 2 hdc, hdc in each ch and in each hdc across: 67{75-83-91} hdc and one ch-3 sp.

Row 5: Ch 2, turn; hdc2tog, hdc in each hdc across to center ch-3, hdc in next ch, 2 hdc in next ch, place marker in last hdc made, hdc in next ch and in each hdc across: 70{78-86-94} hdc.

Row 6: Ch 4 **(counts as first tr, now and throughout)**, turn; tr in next hdc and in each hdc across to marked hdc, 3 tr in marked hdc moving marker to center tr, tr in next hdc and in each hdc across: 72{80-88-96} tr.

Row 7: Ch 4, turn; work FPtr around next tr and around each tr across moving marker up.

Row 8: Ch 2, turn; hdc2tog, hdc in each FPtr across to marked st, 2 hdc in marked st moving marker to last hdc made, hdc in each FPtr across.

Row 9: Ch 2, turn; hdc2tog, ch 2, (skip next 2 hdc, hdc in next 2 hdc, ch 2) 7{8-9-10} times, skip next 2 hdc, hdc in each hdc across to marked hdc, 2 hdc in marked hdc moving marker to last hdc made, hdc in each hdc across to last 32{36-40-44} hdc, (ch 2, skip next 2 hdc, hdc in next 2 hdc) across.

Rows 10 and 11: Ch 2, turn; hdc2tog, hdc in each st across to marked hdc, 2 hdc in marked hdc moving marker to last hdc made, hdc in each st across.

Repeat Rows 6-11, 6{6-7-7} times, adding 2 sts to the stitch count on each Row 6: 84{92-102-110} hdc.

Finish off; remove marker.

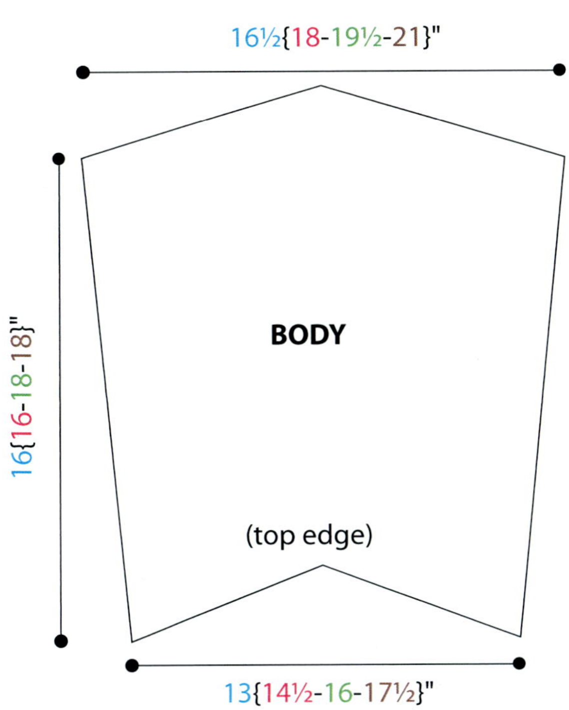

FINISHING

SIDE SEAMS

With **right** sides of both Body pieces together and working through end of rows of **both** pieces, join yarn with slip st in last row made; slip st evenly across leaving last 7{7½-8-8½}"/ 18{19-20.5-21.5} cm unworked for armhole.

Repeat on second side.

NECK EDGING

With **right** side facing and working in free loops of beginning ch ***(Fig. 3, page 30)***, join yarn with slip st in last ch on either Body; slip st in first 2{2-1-2} ch(s) on second Body to join shoulder, (ch 2, slip st in second ch from hook and in next 3 chs) across both pieces and joining second shoulder in same manner, to last 1{0-0-1} ch(s) ***(see Zeros, page 29)***, ch 2, slip st in second ch from hook and in last 1{0-0-1} ch(s); join with slip st to joining slip st, finish off.

ARMHOLE EDGING

Rnd 1: With **right** side facing and working in end of rows, join yarn with sc in first row after side seam ***(see Joining With Sc, page 30)***; sc evenly around armhole working a multiple of 3 sc; join with slip st to first sc.

Rnd 2: Slip st in next sc, (ch 2, slip st in second ch from hook and in next 3 sc) around to last sc, ch 2, slip st in second ch from hook and in last sc; join with slip st to joining slip st, finish off.

Repeat for second Armhole.

BOTTOM EDGING

Rnd 1: With **right** side facing, join yarn with sc in first hdc on either Body; ch 3, skip next 3 hdc, (sc in next hdc, ch 3, skip next 3 hdc) around; join with slip st to first sc.

Rnd 2: Ch 1, sc in same st as joining, ch 6, (sc in next sc, ch 6) around; join with slip st to first sc.

Rnd 3: ★ 5 Sc in next ch-6 sp, ch 2, slip st in second ch from hook, 4 sc in same sp, slip st in next sc; repeat from ★ around working last slip st in joining slip st, finish off.

Kaleidoscope

This bohemian item reinvents the granny square into something utterly fresh and exciting: a fitted vest that lies beautifully and buttons off to the side. The fringe along the hem adds a playful touch.

SHOPPING LIST

EASY

Yarn (Light Weight) 3

[3.5 ounces, 306 yards (100 grams, 280 meters) per skein]:

- ☐ Color A (Rose) - 1{2} skein(s)
- ☐ Color B (Grey) - 1 skein
- ☐ Color C (Dark Grey) - 1 skein
- ☐ Color D (Light Green) - 1 skein
- ☐ Color E (Green) - 1 skein

Crochet Hook

- ☐ Size Extra Small - Size 7 (4.5 mm)
- ☐ Size Small - Size H (5 mm)
- ☐ Size Medium - Size I (5.5 mm)
- ☐ Size Large - Size 7 (4.5 mm)
- ☐ Size Extra Large - Size H (5 mm)

or size needed for gauge

Additional Supplies

- ☐ Sewing needle and thread
- ☐ ½" (12 mm) Buttons - 5{6}

SIZE INFORMATION

Size	Finished Chest Measurement
Extra Small	30" (76 cm)
Small	33" (84 cm)
Medium	36" (91.5 cm)
Large	40" (101.5 cm)
Extra Large	44" (112 cm)

Size Note: We have printed the instructions for the sizes in different colors to make it easier for you to find:

- Sizes Extra Small, Small, & Medium in Blue
- Sizes Large, & Extra Large in Pink

Instructions in Black apply to all sizes.

GAUGE INFORMATION

The Motifs are worked the same for all sizes. Final measurement is obtained by using a different hook size as recommended under Shopping List **and** acheiving the gauge specified below.

Sizes Extra Small & Large:
One Motif = 2" (5 cm) square

Sizes Small & Extra Large:
One Motif = 2¼" (5.75 cm) square

Size Medium:
One Motif = 2½" (6.25 cm) square

Make a total of 59{87} Motifs, referring to the following table for how many of each color combination to make and the color of each round.

Make	19{23}	14{18}	16{26}	10{20}
Rnd	**Motif 1**	**Motif 2**	**Motif 3**	**Motif 4**
1	E	C	B	D
2	B	A	A	C
3	D	B	C	E

MOTIF

With first color, ch 6; join with slip st to form a ring.

Rnd 1 (Right side)**:** Ch 1, (4 sc in ring, ch 1) 4 times; join with slip st to first sc, finish off: 16 sc and 4 ch-1 sps.

Note: Loop a short piece of yarn around any stitch to mark Rnd 1 as **right** side.

Rnd 2: With **right** side facing, join next color with dc in any ch-1 sp ***(see Joining With Dc, page 30)***; (2 dc, ch 1, 3 dc) in same sp, ch 1, (3 dc, ch 1) twice in each ch-1 sp around; join with slip st to first dc, finish off: 24 dc and 8 ch-1 sps.

Rnd 3: With **right** side facing, join next color with sc in any corner ch-1 sp ***(see Joining With Sc, page 30)***, 2 sc in same sp, sc in next 3 dc, sc in next ch-1 sp and in next 3 dc, ★ 3 sc in next corner ch-1 sp, sc in next 3 dc, sc in next ch-1 sp and in next 3 dc; repeat from ★ 2 times **more**; join with slip st to first sc, finish off: 40 sc.

TRIANGLE

Color Combo #1 - Make 2 in the following color sequence: Color D, Color C, Color E.

Color Combo #4 - Make 2{4} in the following color sequence: Color C, Color A, Color B.

With first color, ch 6; join with slip st to form a ring.

Row 1 (Right side)**:** Ch 1, (4 sc, ch 1, 4 sc) in ring; do **not** join, finish off: 8 sc and 1 ch-1 sp.

Note: Mark Row 1 as **right** side.

Row 2: With **right** side facing, join next color with dc in first sc; 2 dc in same st, ch 1, (3 dc, ch 1) twice in next ch-1 sp, skip next 3 sc, 3 dc in last sc; finish off: 12 dc and 3 ch-1 sps.

Last Rnd: With **right** side facing, join next color with sc in first dc; 2 sc in same st, sc in next 2 dc, sc in next ch-1 sp and in next 3 dc, 3 sc in next corner ch-1 sp, sc in next 3 dc, sc in next ch-1 sp and in next 2 dc, 3 sc in last dc, work 9 sc evenly spaced across end of rows and in beginning ring; join with slip st to first sc, finish off: 30 sc.

ASSEMBLY

Block Motifs to gauge ***(see Blocking, page 31)***.

FIRST MOTIF EDGING

Using Placement Diagram as a guide, work the Motif Edging around the left hand bottom corner Motif.

With **right** side facing and working in Back Loops Only ***(Fig. 2, page 30)***, join Color A with slip st in center sc of any corner 3-sc group; ch 3, slip st in same st, ch 3, (skip next sc, slip st in next sc, ch 3) 4 times, skip next sc, ★ (slip st, ch 3) twice in next sc, (skip next sc, slip st in next sc, ch 3) 4 times, skip next sc; repeat from ★ 2 times **more**; join with slip st to joining slip st, finish off.

The method used to connect the Motifs is a no-sew joining also known as "join-as-you-go." The Motifs are crocheted together as the Edging is worked. Holding pieces with **wrong** sides together, slip st in space as indicated ***(Fig. A, page 14)***.

ONE SIDE JOINING

With **right** side facing and working in Back Loops Only of next Motif, join Color A with slip st in center sc of any corner 3-sc group; ch 3, (skip next sc, slip st in next sc, ch 3) 4 times, ★ skip next sc, (slip st, ch 3) twice in next sc, (skip next sc, slip st in next sc, ch 3) 4 times; repeat from ★ once **more**, skip next sc, slip st in next sc, ch 1, slip st in corresponding ch-3 sp on **adjacent Motif**, ch 1, slip st in same sc on **new Motif**, ch 1, slip st in center ch of next ch-3 on **adjacent Motif**, ch 1, † skip next sc on **new Motif**, slip st in next sc, ch 1, slip st in center ch of next ch-3 on **adjacent Motif**, ch 1 †; repeat from † to † 3 times **more**, skip next sc on **new Motif**, slip st in same st as joining, ch 1, slip st in next ch-3 sp on **previous Motif**, ch 1; join with slip st to joining slip st, finish off.

When joining to a previously joined corner, slip st in same space.

TWO SIDE JOINING

With **right** side facing and working in Back Loops Only of next Motif, join Color A with slip st in center sc of any corner 3-sc group; ch 3, (skip next sc, slip st in next sc, ch 3) 4 times, skip next sc, (slip st, ch 3) twice in next sc, (skip next sc, slip st in next sc, ch 3) 4 times; skip next sc, ★ slip st in next sc, ch 1, slip st in corresponding ch-3 sp on **adjacent Motif**, ch 1, slip st in same sc on **new Motif**, ch 1, slip st in center ch of next ch-3 on **adjacent Motif**, ch 1, † skip next sc on **new Motif**, slip st in next sc, ch 1, slip st in center ch of next ch-3 on **adjacent Motif**, ch 1 †; repeat from † to † 3 times **more**, skip next sc on **new Motif**; repeat from ★ once **more**, slip st in same st as joining, ch 1, slip st in next ch-3 sp on **adjacent Motif**, ch 1; join with slip st to joining slip st, finish off.

TWO OPPOSITE SIDES JOINING

With **right** side facing and working in Back Loops Only of next Motif, join Color A with slip st in center sc of any corner 3-sc group; ★ (ch 3, skip next sc, slip st in next sc) 5 times, ch 1, slip st in corresponding ch-3 sp on **adjacent Motif**, ch 1, slip st in same sc on **new Motif**, † ch 1, slip st in center ch of next ch-3 on **adjacent Motif**, ch 1, skip next sc on **new Motif**, slip st in next sc †; repeat from † to † 4 times **more**, ch 1, slip st in next ch-3 sp on **adjacent Motif**, ch 1, slip st in same sc on **new Motif**; repeat from ★ once **more** ending by working last slip st in joining slip st, finish off.

PLACEMENT DIAGRAMS

EXTRA SMALL, SMALL, & MEDIUM

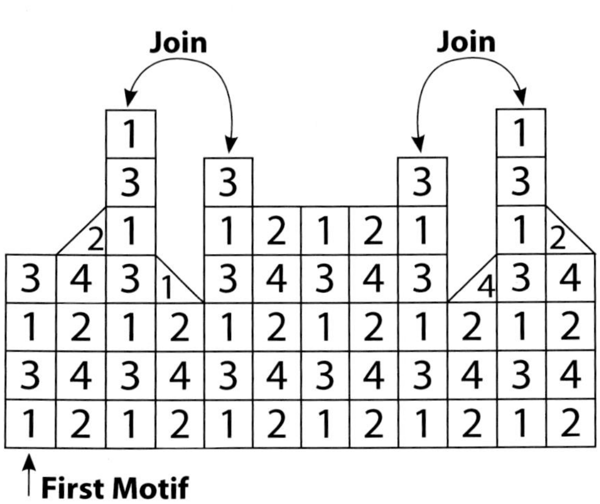

LARGE & EXTRA LARGE

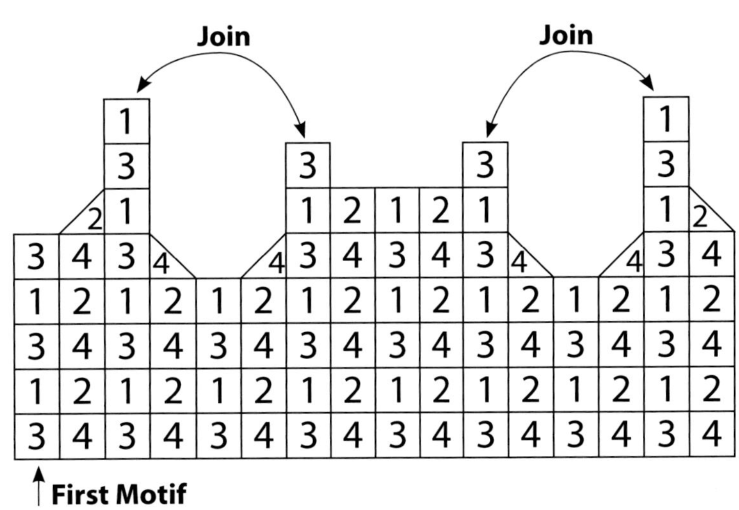

TRIANGLE JOINING

With **right** side facing and working in Back Loops Only, join Color A with slip st in sc after last corner 3-sc group made on Triangle; (ch 3, skip next sc, slip st in next sc) 5 times, ch 1, slip st in corresponding ch-3 sp on **previous Motif**, ch 1, slip st in same sc on **new Motif**, ★ ch 1, slip st in center ch of next ch-3 on **previous Motif**, ch 1, slip st in next sc on **new Motif**, † ch 1, slip st in center ch of next ch-3 on **previous Motif**, ch 1, skip next sc on **new Motif**, slip st in next sc †; repeat from † to † 3 times **more,** ch 1, slip st in next ch-3 sp on **previous Motif**, ch 1, slip st in same sc on **new Motif**; repeat from ★ once **more**, ch 3, skip last sc; join with slip st to joining slip st, finish off.

FINISHING

FRONT EDGING

With **right** side facing, join Color C with slip st in center ch of bottom corner ch-3 on Right Front; (ch 3, (slip st in center ch of next ch-3) around entire piece; join with slip st to joining slip st, finish off.

ARMHOLE EDGING

With **right** side facing, join Color C with slip st in center ch of any ch-3 on armhole; ch 3, (slip st in center ch of next ch-3, ch 3) around; join with slip st to joining slip st, finish off.

Repeat for second Armhole.

Block vest to finished measurement.

FRINGE

Holding three, 12" (30.5 cm) strands of yarn together, add fringe in each ch-3 sp across bottom edge ***(Figs. 7a & b, page 31)***, alternating Color B, Color A, and Color C.

Using photo as a guide for placement, sew buttons to Right Front at corners of Motifs.
Uses spaces on Left Front as buttonholes.

General Instructions

ABBREVIATIONS

ch(s)	chain(s)
cm	centimeters
dc	double crochet(s)
dc2tog	double crochet(s) 2 together
FPtr	Front Post treble crochet(s)
hdc	half double crochet(s)
hdc2tog	half double crochet 2 together
mm	millimeters
Rnd(s)	Round(s)
sc	single crochet(s)
sc2tog	single crochet 2 together
sp(s)	space(s)
st(s)	stitch(es)
tr	treble crochet(s)
YO	yarn over

SYMBOLS & TERMS

★ — work instructions following ★ as many **more** times as indicated in addition to the first time.

† to † — work all instructions from first † to second † **as many** times as specified.

( ) or [ ] — work enclosed instructions **as many** times as specified by the number immediately following **or** work all enclosed instructions in the stitch or space indicated **or** contains explanatory remarks.

colon (:) — the number(s) given after a colon at the end of a row or round denote(s) the number of stitches or spaces you should have on that row or round.

work even — work without increasing or decreasing in the established pattern.

GAUGE

Exact gauge is **essential** for proper fit. Before beginning your project, make the sample swatch given in the individual instructions in the yarn and hook specified. After completing the swatch, measure it, counting your stitches and rows/rounds carefully. If your swatch is larger or smaller than specified, **make another, changing hook size to get the correct gauge.** Keep trying until you find the size hook that will give you the specified gauge.

ZEROS

To consolidate the length of an involved pattern, zeros are sometimes used so that all sizes can be combined. For example, work across to last 1{0-0-1} st(s) means the first and last sizes work across to last st and the second and third sizes do nothing.

CROCHET TERMINOLOGY		
UNITED STATES		INTERNATIONAL
slip stitch (slip st)	=	single crochet (sc)
single crochet (sc)	=	double crochet (dc)
half double crochet (hdc)	=	half treble crochet (htr)
double crochet (dc)	=	treble crochet (tr)
treble crochet (tr)	=	double treble crochet (dtr)
double treble crochet (dtr)	=	triple treble crochet (ttr)
triple treble crochet (tr tr)	=	quadruple treble crochet (qtr)
skip	=	miss

CROCHET HOOKS																	
U.S.	B-1	C-2	D-3	E-4	F-5	G-6	7	H-8	I-9	J-10	K-10½	L-11	M/N-13	N/P-15	P/Q	Q	S
Metric - mm	2.25	2.75	3.25	3.5	3.75	4	4.5	5	5.5	6	6.5	8	9	10	15	16	19

BEGINNER	Projects for first-time crocheters using basic stitches. Minimal shaping.
EASY	Projects using yarn with basic stitches, repetitive stitch patterns, simple color changes, and simple shaping and finishing.
INTERMEDIATE	Projects using a variety of techniques, such as basic lace patterns or color patterns, mid-level shaping and finishing.
EXPERIENCED	Projects with intricate stitch patterns, techniques and dimension, such as non-repeating patterns, multi-color techniques, fine threads, small hooks, detailed shaping and refined finishing.

JOINING WITH SC

When instructed to join with sc, begin with a slip knot on hook. Insert hook in stitch or space indicated, YO and pull up a loop, YO and draw through both loops on hook.

JOINING WITH DC

When instructed to join with dc, begin with a slip knot on hook. YO, holding loop on hook, insert hook in stitch or space indicated, YO and pull up a loop (3 loops on hook), (YO and draw through 2 loops on hook) twice.

BACK RIDGE

Work only in loops indicated by arrows *(Fig. 1)*.

Fig. 1

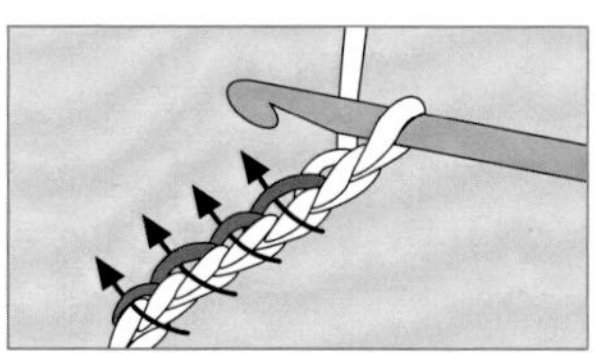

BACK OR FRONT LOOP ONLY

Work only in loop(s) indicated by arrow *(Fig. 2)*.

Fig. 2

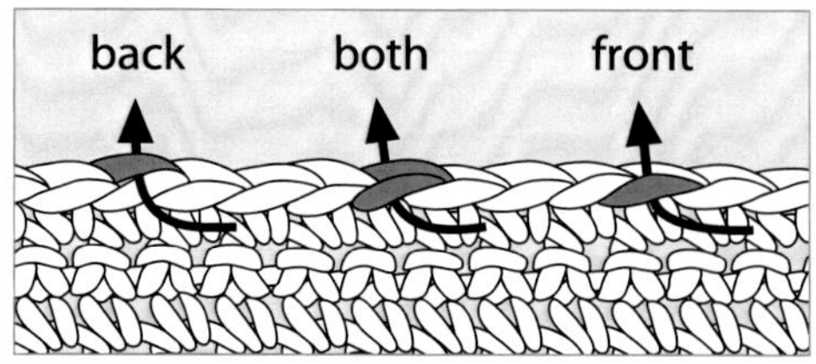

FREE LOOPS OF A CHAIN

When instructed to work in free loops of a chain, work in loop indicated by arrow *(Fig. 3)*.

Fig. 3

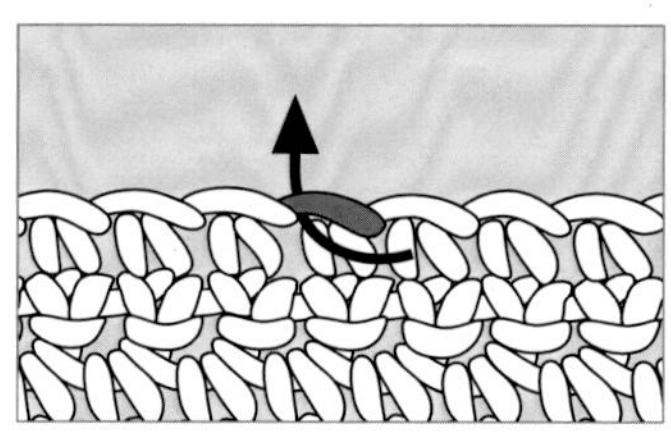

POST STITCH

Work around post of stitch indicated, inserting hook in direction of arrow *(Fig. 4)*.

Fig. 4

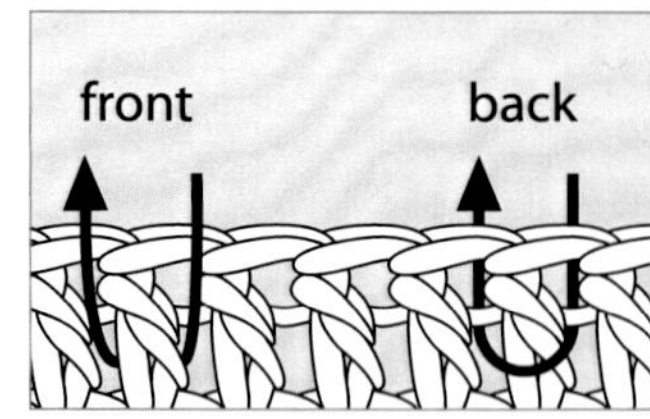

WHIPSTITCH

With **wrong** sides together, sew through both pieces once to secure the beginning of the seam, leaving an ample yarn end to weave in later. Insert the needle from **right** to **left** through two strands on each stitch on each piece ***(Fig. 5a)* or** through ends of rows *(Fig. 5b)*. Bring the needle around and insert it from **right** to **left** through the next strands on both pieces.

Repeat along the edge, being careful to match stitches and rows.

Fig. 5a

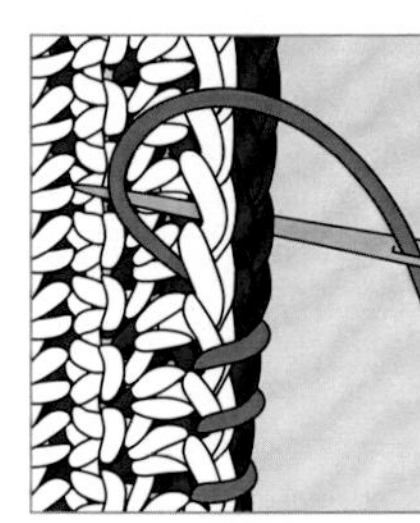

Fig. 5b

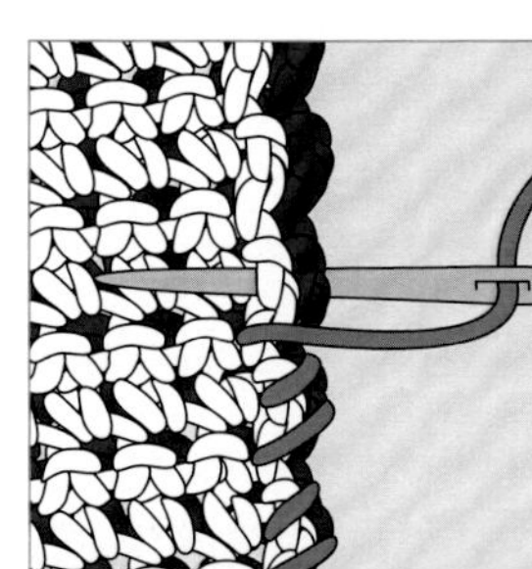

Yarn Weight Symbol & Names	LACE 0	SUPER FINE 1	FINE 2	LIGHT 3	MEDIUM 4	BULKY 5	SUPER BULKY 6	JUMBO 7
Type of Yarns in Category	Fingering, size 10 crochet thread	Sock, Fingering, Baby	Sport, Baby	DK, Light Worsted	Worsted, Afghan, Aran	Chunky, Craft, Rug	Super Bulky, Roving	Jumbo, Roving
Crochet Gauge* Ranges in Single Crochet to 4" (10 cm)	32-42 sts**	21-32 sts	16-20 sts	12-17 sts	11-14 sts	8-11 sts	6-9 sts	5 sts and fewer
Advised Hook Size Range	Steel*** 6 to 8, Regular hook B-1	B-1 to E-4	E-4 to 7	7 to I-9	I-9 to K-10½	K-10½ to M/N-13	M/N-13 to Q	Q and larger

*GUIDELINES ONLY: The chart above reflects the most commonly used gauges and hook sizes for specific yarn categories.

** Lace weight yarns are usually crocheted with larger hooks to create lacy openwork patterns. Accordingly, a gauge range is difficult to determine. Always follow the gauge stated in your pattern.

*** Steel crochet hooks are sized differently from regular hooks–the higher the number, the smaller the hook, which is the reverse of regular hook sizing.

MATTRESS STITCH

With the **right** sides of both edges facing you and matching sts, sew through both sides once to secure the seam, leaving an ample yarn end to weave in later. Insert the needle from **right** to **left** through strand on one side ***(Fig. 6a)***, then from **left** to **right** on the other side ***(Fig. 6b)***. Continue in this manner, drawing seam together as you work. This will create a flat seam.

FRINGE

Cut a piece of cardboard 5" (12.5 cm) wide and half as long as the strands specified in individual instructions. Wind the yarn loosely and evenly lengthwise around the cardboard until the card is filled, then cut across one end; repeat as needed.

Hold together as many strands as specified in individual instructions; fold in half.

With **wrong** side facing and using a crochet hook, draw the folded end up through a space and pull the loose ends through the folded end ***(Fig. 7a)***; draw the knot up tightly ***(Fig. 7b)***. Repeat, spacing as specified in individual instructions.

Lay flat on a hard surface and trim the ends.

Fig. 6a

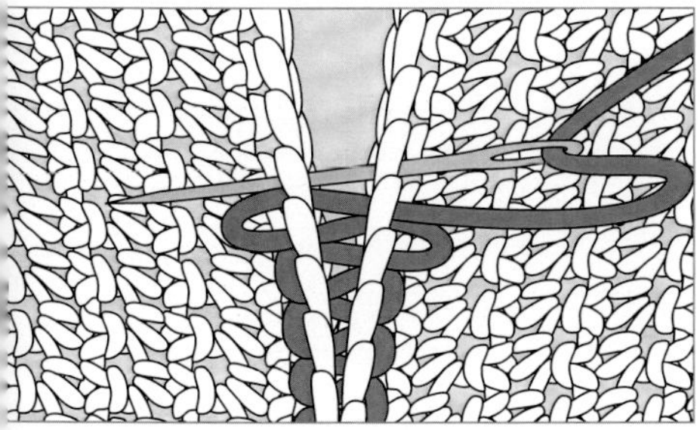

Fig. 6b

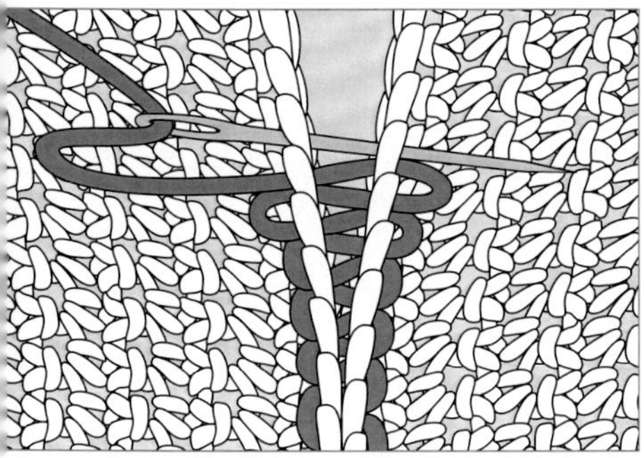

Fig. 7a

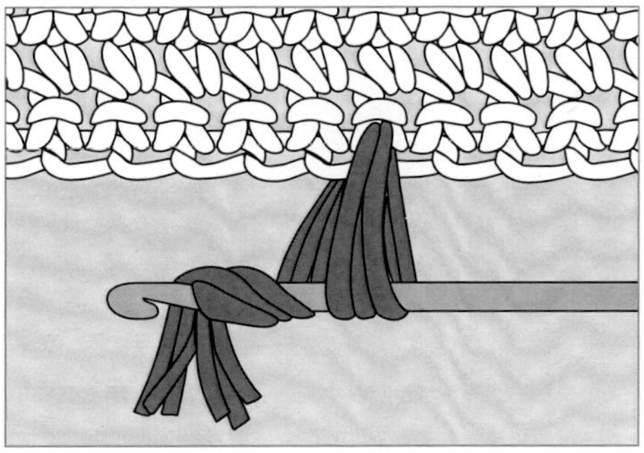

Fig. 7b

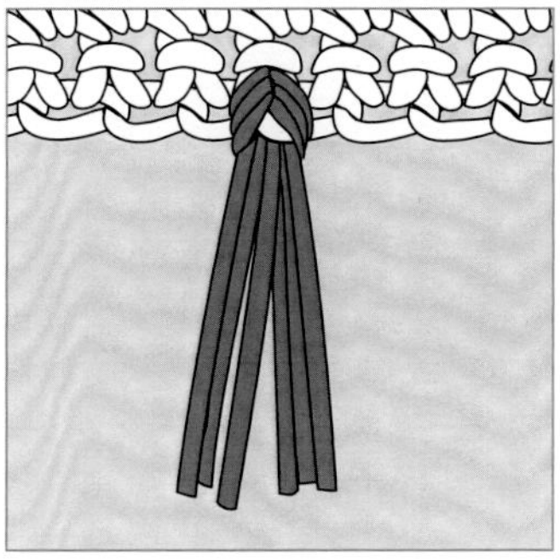

BLOCKING

Follow instructions on yarn label or block as follows:

Wool: Steam vest, supporting weight of iron at all times. Allow to dry flat, away from heat or sunlight.

Synthetic and blends: Submerge vest in cool water. Roll piece in a clean terry towel and gently press out the excess moisture. Lay vest flat and allow to dry completely, away from heat and sunlight.

YARN INFORMATION

The vests in this book were made using Light and Bulky Weight yarns. Any brand of the specific weight of yarn may be used. It is best to refer to the yardage/meters when determining how many balls or skeins to purchase. Remember, to arrive at the finished size, it is the GAUGE/TENSION that is important, not the brand of yarn.

For your convenience, listed below are the yarns used to create our photography models. Because yarn manufacturers make frequent changes in their product lines, you may sometimes find it necessary to use a substitute yarn or to search for the discontinued product at alternate suppliers (locally or online).

Fjord Lace
Patons® Grace™
Main Color - #62008 Natural
Color A - #62110 Navy
Color B - #62416 Blush

Cherry Schwinn
Patons® Astra™
#08436 Cherry

Irish Mist
Mary Maxim® Northland Yarns Chunky
#001 Grey Marl

Café Au Lait Cable Wrap
Bernat® Roving™
#00011 Bark

Starbusrt Duster
Patons® Silk Bamboo™
#85008 Ivory

Tidal Wave
Mary Maxim® Fresh
#707 Cool Waters

Kaleidoscope
LB Collection® Superwash Merino
Rose - #135 Persimmon
Grey - #123 Hemp
Dark Grey - #149 Charcoal
Light Green - #194 Acid Green
Green - #174 Spring Leaf

We have made every effort to ensure that these instructions are accurate and complete. We cannot, however, be responsible for human error, typographical mistakes, or variations in individual work.

Production Team: Instructional/Technical Editor - Cathy Hardy; Editorial Writer - Susan Frantz Wiles; Graphic Artist - Kytanna McFarlin; Senior Graphic Artist - Lora Puls; Photo Stylist - Lori Wenger; and Photographer - Jason Masters.

Made In U.S.A.

Meet Abbey Swanson

A designer and artist, Abbey Swanson is passionate about crochet that is functional, wearable, and gorgeous. "I am inspired by the beauty found both in nature and in architecture and love seeing how specific elements and color schemes translate to a pattern," she says. Abbey discovered her love for designing crochet after she made an owl hat for her son and then began designing hats for craft fairs.

"I love making items that are elegant yet simple to create," she says. Teaching crochet classes has helped her become attuned to what makes sense to crocheters at various skill levels. "I think this is a major reason my designs aren't overly complicated."

Abbey says her mission is to motivate a new generation of crocheters with designs that move beyond the granny square into a new and fresh reputation for crochet. More about Abbey and her business, The Firefly Hook, may be found at thefireflyhook.wordpress.com or on Etsy, Ravelry, Craftsy, and Facebook.

Abbey and her husband live with their three "wildly energetic and creative children" in a bustling lake town near Minneapolis, Minnesota. "My husband and I enjoy exploring with them on nature walks and fostering a love of learning in our home."